D0532642

THE ZOMBIE COMBAT FIELD GUIDE

A COLOURING AND ACTIVITY BOOK FOR FIGHTING THE LIVING DEAD

ROGER MA

Illustrations by Y. N. Heller

Michael O'Mara Books Limited

First published in Great Britain in 2015 by
Michael O'Mara Books Limited
9 Lion Yard
Tremadoc Road
London SW4 7NQ

First published in the United States of America by The Berkley Publishing Group, 2015

Copyright © Roger Ma, 2015

All rights reserved. You may not copy, store, distribute, transmit, reproduce or otherwise
make available this publication (or any part of it) in any form, or by any means (electronic,
digital, optical, mechanical, photocopying, recording or otherwise), without the prior written
permission of the publisher. Any person who does any unauthorized act in relation to this
publication may be liable to criminal prosecution and civil claims for damages.

A CIP catalogue record for this book is available from the British Library.

Papers used by Michael O'Mara Books Limited are natural, recyclable products made from
wood grown in sustainable forests. The manufacturing processes conform to the environmental
regulations of the country of origin.

ISBN: 978-1-78243-425-2 in paperback print format

1 2 3 4 5 6 7 8 9 10

www.mombooks.com

Illustrated by Y. N. Heller
Interior text design by Tiffany Estreicher

Printed and bound in China

INTRODUCTION

"Just shoot 'em in the head." This is often the first and only recommendation provided when you are confronted by a member of the living dead. The common solution to eliminating a zombie is a bullet to the brain. Unfortunately, this limited piece of advice is not practical for many of us, nor helpful in various situations. What if you do not own a gun? What if you run out of ammunition? What if the sound of the discharge draws more undead creatures your way? This is precisely what my first book, *The Zombie Combat Manual: A Guide to Fighting the Living Dead*, strove to address.

The Zombie Combat Field Guide is a version of that educational text, containing much of the guidance I provided in the original work, but in a versatile, more portable format. Contained within are exercises, fighting techniques, weapon analyses, and battle strategies to confront the living dead in hand-to-hand combat. In addition, activities are included to assist in your retention of the material and to help you create a plan to address the inevitability of an undead infestation.

Another essential element to the usefulness of this work is how you share it with your family. Part of your responsibility as a parent is to protect your loved ones from the clutches of a flesh-hungry ghoul. It is my hope that the following challenges and activities enable you to introduce the idea of a world filled with walking corpses to your entire family as you prepare to defeat them.

Study hard. Keep training. Stay vigilant.

WARNING!

The combat tips and techniques detailed within this field manual are meant to be used solely against members of the living dead. Executing them against living human opponents would not only be immoral but may be ineffective, as they take advantage of weaknesses and traits exhibited by the undead. Do not use them against friends, colleagues, siblings, or other family members, unless you are absolutely certain that they have turned and have joined the ranks of the undead.

UNDEAD PRIMARY ATTACK: THE MOUTH

The mouth is the zombie's primary means of attack. A hungry ghoul will always look first to pull you into its gaping maw. Your initial defence must be to neutralize this means of attack.

UNDEAD SECONDARY ATTACK: THE HANDS

In terms of contamination rate, a ghoul's hands are nearly as hazardous as its mouth. One tiny scratch from a rotten fingernail may spell infection, death, and reanimation. Be wary of the creature's out-stretched claws, particularly during close combat.

UNDEAD TERTIARY ATTACK: ODOUR

The living dead attack not just with their hands and teeth. The foul stench of rotting, sunbaked flesh may render you completely incapacitated if you are not prepared for it.

UNDEAD VULNERABILITIES: THE ZOMBIE SKULL

Neutralizing a zombie is more than just "busting its head". Certain regions of the skull are more vulnerable to compound fracture than others. Study these targets closely; these areas represent the most vulnerable regions of the undead cranium, and are ripe for attack.

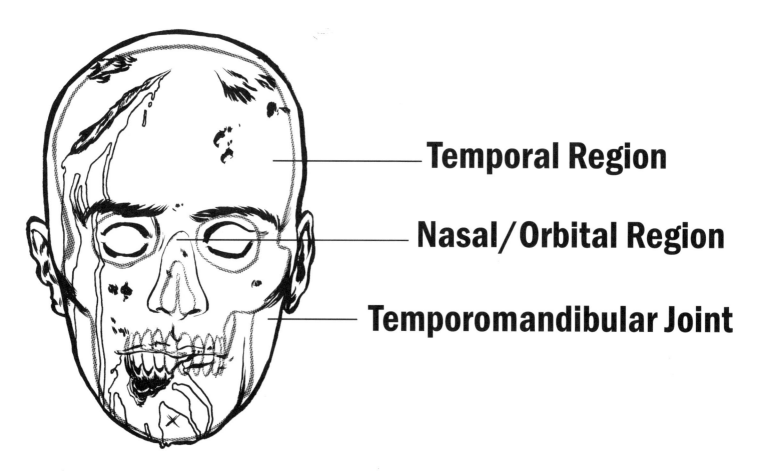

Temporal Region

Nasal/Orbital Region

Temporomandibular Joint

PRIMARY ATTACK TARGET: THE ZOMBIE BRAIN

During your offensive attack, it is not enough to simply crack the zombie skull. You must cause a depressive fracture severe enough to penetrate the grey matter, ideally deep into the white matter of the brain. Make your strikes count!

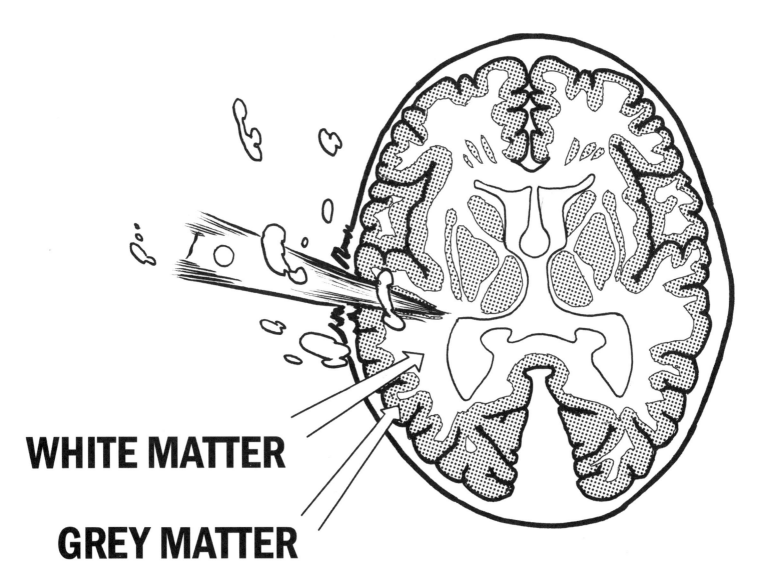

WHITE MATTER

GREY MATTER

KNOW YOUR BLADES

Different types of edged weapons are more effective against certain targets on the zombie skull. Draw a line from the weapon to the appropriate undead target area.[*]

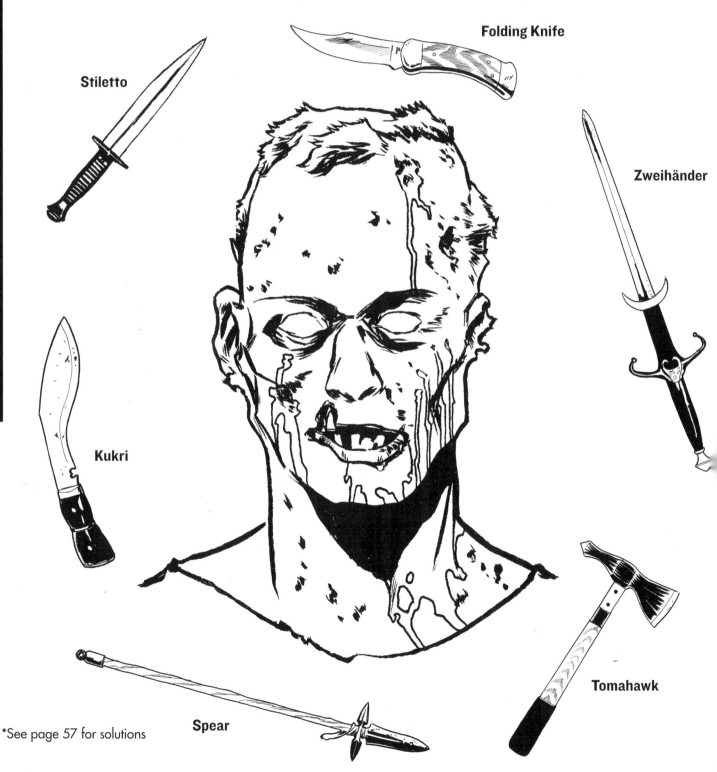

Folding Knife

Stiletto

Zweihänder

Kukri

Tomahawk

Spear

*See page 57 for solutions

COMBATANT, KNOW THYSELF.

Which of these traits do you have that make you an effective zombie combatant?

- ❑ strength
- ❑ martial artist
- ❑ agility
- ❑ outdoorsperson
- ❑ speed

- ❑ low maintenance
- ❑ green thumb
- ❑ country-dweller
- ❑ knowledge of automobiles

Which of these traits make you a liability during an undead outbreak?

- ❑ overweight
- ❑ city-dweller
- ❑ pacifist
- ❑ inflexible
- ❑ poor health

- ❑ lack of endurance
- ❑ white-collar professional
- ❑ high maintenance
- ❑ perfectionist

IMPROVISED WEAPONS

Zombie weapons can be found in all walks of life. Look at these typical household items. Where could you find each if you lost your primary weapon?

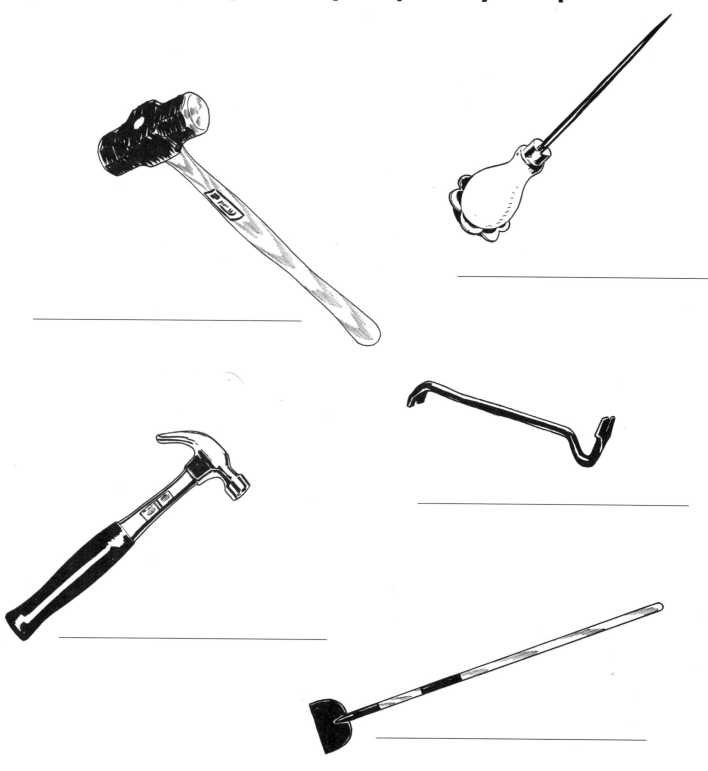

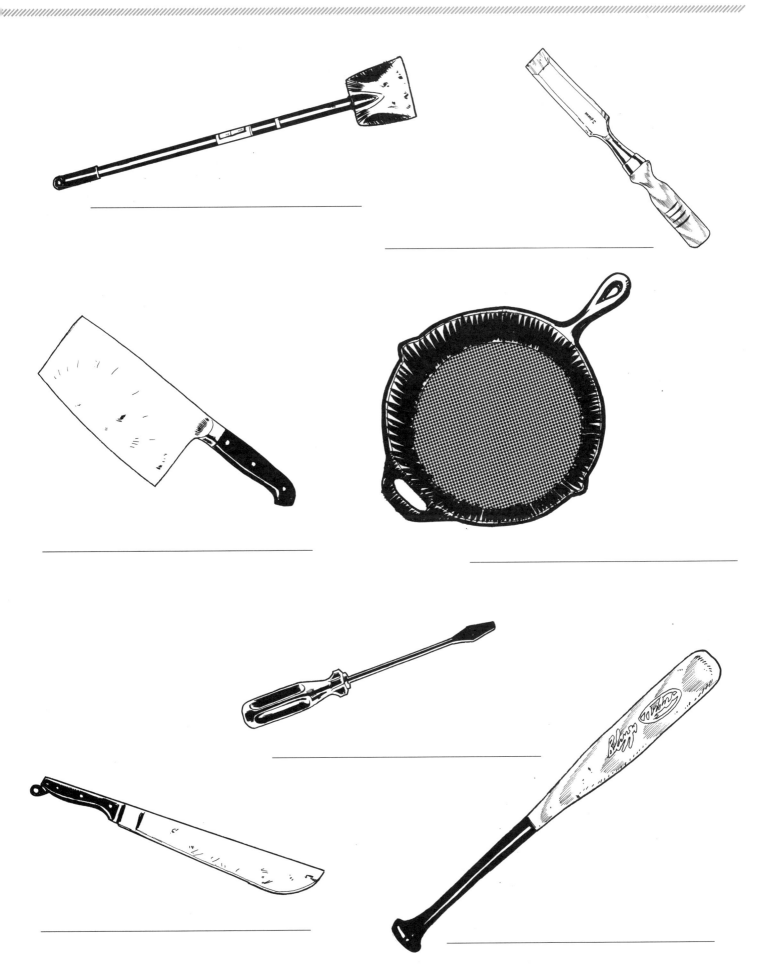

_____

_____

_____

_____

_____

_____

COMBATANT ASSESSMENT: WOULD YOU RATHER?

Would you rather face off against a zombie:

in the water	or	in the dark
using a tennis shoe	or	a tennis racquet
on city streets	or	in the woods
in a beauty parlour	or	in a toy store
who was once someone you knew	or	who was once a celebrity
with a baby on your back	or	with a baby in a sling
who has no arms	or	who has no legs

COMBATANT ASSESSMENT: WHICH ARE YOU?

1. **Of the following, which is your strongest skill in an undead combat situation:**
   a. speed
   b. strength
   c. cardiovascular endurance
   d. training and skill set

2. **Which is your greatest weakness:**
   a. weak muscles
   b. slow speed
   c. poor endurance
   d. I have no weaknesses

3. **Describe your body type:**
   a. lean and compact
   b. thick and heavy
   c. muscular and athletic
   d. superhero

4. **Look around the room you are in. If a zombie attacked right now, which of the following would be your immediate instinct:**
   a. Escape and Evade: Get as much space between myself and the ghoul as possible.
   b. Bum Rush: Quickly overpower the undead assailant with brute force.
   c. Assess and Act: Evaluate the situation for the best solution based on the environment, risks, and tools I have at my disposal.
   d. Trick question—My exterior defences would have alerted me to the presence of a zombie before it entered my immediate vicinity.

Mostly As: You are an Ectocombatant. You prioritize keeping your distance from your undead opponent, and you have the speed to do it. You should avoid close combat if possible. If you are caught in a situation where you cannot outrun the ghoul, your ideal weapon would be a long-range weapon, a spear, or a polearm. In a pinch, a sidewalk scraper will do.

Mostly Bs: You are an Endocombatant. Size and force are on your side, but speed is not, so you may find yourself up close and personal with a zombie in melee range or hand-to-hand combat. Arm yourself with a medieval mace for medium-range undead combat and a combat knife for when things get intimate. In a pinch, use that strength and grab a sledgehammer.

Mostly Cs: You are a Mesocombatant. You possess what is often most desired in combatants: an equal mix of strength, endurance, and speed. Your athletic abilities enable you to adapt to a variety of scenarios equally well. As you possess a balanced skill set, ensure that your arsenal affords you a variety of attack options: short-, medium-, and long-range; a close-combat trench blade; a medium-range crowbar; and a long-range halberd.

Mostly Ds: You are a UCEC: Undead Combatant—Elite Class. Not only do you possess keen physical attributes, you have already prepared for the coming of the living dead. There is no need to advise you on which weapons to choose, as in all likelihood, you have already chosen and trained with them for hours on end.

ZOMBIE FIGHTING PHYSIQUE: THE MESOCOMBATANT

THE MESOCOMBATANT

Traits: Athletic, solid musculature

Strengths: Balanced levels of strength and speed

Liabilities: Lower body-fat levels

ZOMBIE FIGHTING PHYSIQUE: THE ECTOCOMBATANT

THE ECTOCOMBATANT

Traits: Lean, light musculature

Strengths: Endurance, speed, stealth

Liabilities: Lack of strength and power, extremely low body fat

ZOMBIE FIGHTING PHYSIQUE: THE ENDOCOMBATANT

THE ENDOCOMBATANT

Traits: Heavier build, round physique

Strengths: Energy storage, power, leverage

Liabilities: Lack of speed and endurance

PHYSICAL CONDITIONING: SKULLPOPPERS

Incorporate exercises into your fitness routine that simulate actions you may have to perform during a combat engagement. One such exercise is the Skullpopper. Building strength in this movement will help when you must finish a fallen or decapitated zombie with the heel of your boot.

1. Place a car tyre on a stable surface.

2. Mark a spot on the tyre.

3. Raise your knee to your chest, then stomp on the mark as forcefully as you can.

4. Repeat for 10 to 20 repetitions per side.

PHYSICAL CONDITIONING: CIRCUIT TRAINING

Every zombie combatant should be ready to engage in undead combat at a moment's notice. Conditioning is key to your success in conflict against a walking corpse. How many times can you complete the basic fitness circuit on the following pages?

ZOMBIE BASIC FITNESS CIRCUIT:

- 20 push-ups

- 20 burpees

- 10 box jumps (or 20 jumping jacks, should a box be unavailable)

- 10 pull-ups

- 20 squats

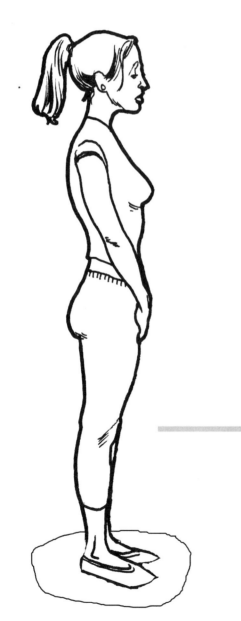

CHILD PROTECTION: TRANSPORTING CHILDREN DURING AN UNDEAD OUTBREAK

If you need to evacuate a safe zone with your infant, make sure you have a comfortable carrier to keep your hands free to ready your weapon. Some good options are:

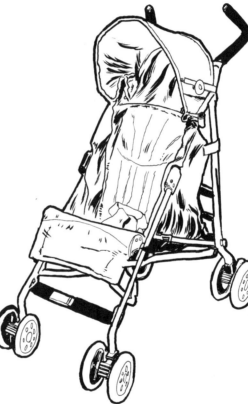

PUSHCHAIR

Advantages: Long-distance travel, minimal energy expenditure

Disadvantages: Heavy, inflexible, potential separation from direct contact with child

SLING

Advantages: Light, inexpensive, portable, low child position on the body away from zombie jaws

Disadvantages: Protector bears weight, inappropriate for older children

BACK CARRIER

Advantages: Portable, manoeuvrable, multitasking, limited exposure to frontal attacks

Disadvantages: Limb exposure, weight-bearing, complex mounting, inability to carry supplies on your back, lack of visibility in the event of a rear attack

CHEST CARRIER

Advantages: Portable, manoeuvrable, multitasking, full child visibility at all times

Disadvantages: Limb and head exposure, weight-bearing, complex mounting, vulnerable in frontal assault

WHO WOULD YOU SAVE?

In an undead outbreak, you may have to make some unfortunate decisions, most common being: Who will you save when you cannot save everyone?

Rank the following in order of rescue:

PERSON	RANK	REASON
Mother		
Father		
Sibling		
Spouse		
Children		
Best Friend		
Pet(s)		

WHO'S ON YOUR TEAM?

During a zombie infestation, you may want to assemble a crew of allies to help you fend off and survive the undead. Who among your family, friends, and associates would be in your top five?

TEAMMATE	SKILLS/ASSETS
1.	
2.	
3.	
4.	
5.	

YOUR ZOMBIE GETAWAY KIT

A prepared combatant is a smart combatant. Make a list of the key items you'll need should you have to evacuate your stronghold.

WEAPONS	SUPPLIES	MEDICAL	SHELTER

SUPPLY MISSION

A warehouse stocked with food and supplies sits untouched, a maze of zombie-infested city streets away from your stronghold. Your survival depends on access to these new supplies.

START

WAREHOUSE

ZOMBIE COMBAT TIP: AVOID THE "FATAL FUNNEL"

The most dangerous position you can confront your undead attacker is directly head-on. Avoid the "fatal funnel", the triangular sector comprising a zombie's mouth and outstretched hands, and move around the perimeter of your opponent, using your speed to your advantage in your attack.

ZOMBIE COMBAT TIP: CONTROL THE WEAPON!

In undead close combat, it is critical that you keep the ghoul's jaws at bay. Control its weapon by taking hold of its neck, keeping it away from your flesh.

ZOMBIE COMBAT SCENARIO: THE WALK-IN WARDROBE

On a routine house search, you become momentarily distracted as you open a door in the master bedroom. Cold, dead hands grab your lapels and pull you into the wardrobe where the ghoul was originally trapped. You topple to the floor with the ghoul mounted on top of you, pushing its jaws towards your exposed neck. You are armed with a katana sword, which is sheathed across your back and pressed against the floor.

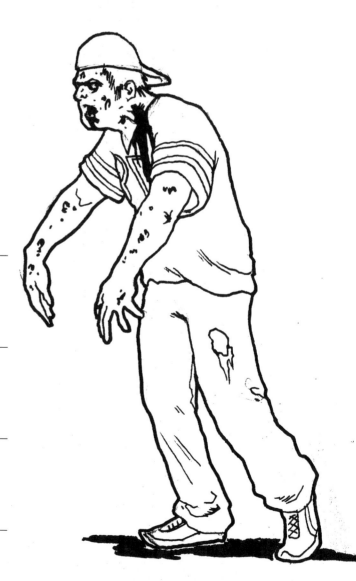

What advantages do you have in this scenario?

_____

What are your disadvantages?

_____

How will you use your primary weapon?

_____

What is your tactical plan?

_____

ZOMBIE COMBAT TIP: NO HAIR PULLING!

A decomposing scalp is liable to come right off in your hand if you attempt to yank your opponent's hair. Remember: An undead head feels no pain.

ZOMBIE COMBAT TIP: UNARMED COMBAT

The most hazardous type of zombie combat is fighting a ghoul unarmed. Remember the following tips:

1. Don't panic.

2. Watch for scratches.

3. End the fight quickly; the longer you battle, the more likely you'll lose.

ZOMBIE COMBAT TIP: FIGHT SMARTER, NOT HARDER

Use your intellect over your strength. Why exert yourself if you don't have to?

ZOMBIE COMBAT SCENARIO: THE APARTMENT COMPLEX

You are on the seventh floor of a fifteen-floor apartment building. Having searched the upper floors and finding no walking corpses, you now find yourself face-to-face with seven ghouls making their way up the building's only staircase (the lifts are out of order). You are aware that the roof door is unlocked. An adjoining building is ten feet from yours. You are armed with a bowie knife.

What advantages do you have in this scenario?

_____

What are your disadvantages?

_____

How will you use your primary weapon?

_____

What is your tactical plan?

_____

ZOMBIE COMBAT TIP: WATCH YOUR GRIP!

In combat, hands may get slippery from sweat, blood, or other undead fluids. Make sure you have a secure grip on your weapon before initiating an attack.

ZOMBIE COMBAT TIP: WEAPON THROWING

As a result of media influence, poor advice, or simple overconfidence, there may come a time when you are tempted to hurl your weapon at a ghoul. This is **NOT RECOMMENDED** for the following reasons:

1. Weapons that are thrown are often specially designed to do so.

2. It takes years of dedicated training to consistently "stick" a weapon in your target.

3. Throwing your weapon means losing your weapon, even if for a moment.

ZOMBIE COMBAT TIP: NIGHT FIGHTING

When fighting in the dark, the zombie has the upper hand. Follow these tips to level the field of combat:

1. Avoid the darkness if at all possible.

2. Let your eyes adjust to night vision before you begin to move.

3. Ready your weapon at all times.

4. Watch your back.

ZOMBIE COMBAT SCENARIO: THE TRAIN

You are on a train that is barrelling through a darkened tunnel when it comes to a screeching halt. The lights in the carriage flicker, then blink off. Minutes pass. In the darkness, you begin to hear moans coming from both ends of the carriage. Screams cut through the silence as ghouls stumble their way in through both doorways. You are carrying a bag of tools including a hammer and a chisel.

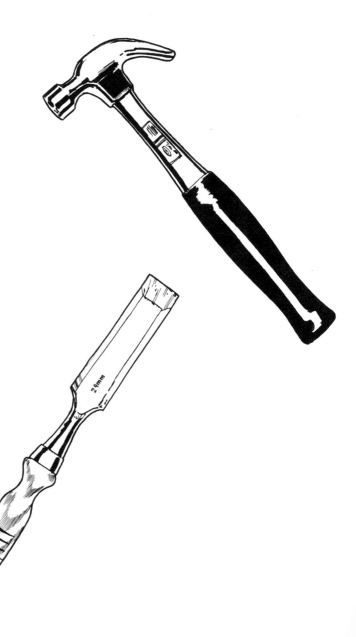

What advantages do you have in this scenario?

_____

What are your disadvantages?

_____

How will you use your primary weapons?

_____

What is your tactical plan?

_____

ZOMBIE COMBAT TIP: AQUATIC COMBAT

Fighting the undead in any type of aquatic setting presents a unique set of challenges not present on dry land. If you must engage a zombie opponent in the water, remember these tips:

1. Take a wide stance to avoid slipping on moss-covered rocks.

2. Keep in mind that your speed is diminished, so avoid close-range combat.

3. Watch for fully submerged ghouls lurking below deep waters.

ZOMBIE COMBAT SCENARIO: THE RIVERSIDE

You have been driven by a mob of twenty zombies to the edge of a riverbed that spans thirty feet. The water looks calm, but you are unsure of its depth. You step into the water and feel a mossy bed of rocks under your feet. You cannot turn back in the same direction due to the approaching horde. The ghouls will be on your position in ten seconds. You are armed with a long staff.

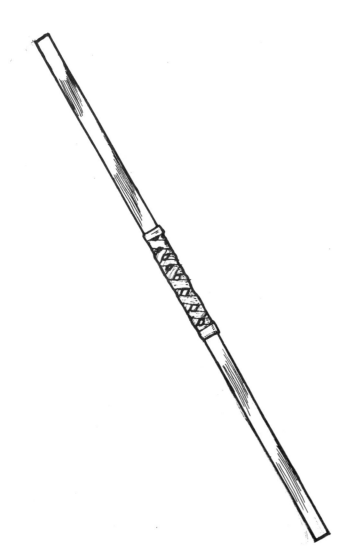

What advantages do you have in this scenario?

_____

What are your disadvantages?

_____

How will you use your primary weapon?

_____

What is your tactical plan?

_____

ZOMBIE COMBAT TIP: GAIN THE HIGH GROUND

Whenever possible, fight from an elevated position, especially when confronted by multiple undead assailants.

ZOMBIE COMBAT SCENARIO: THE CITY

You are in the middle of a downtown business district in the midst of mayhem. The streets are packed with panicked, terror-stricken citizens, unaware that the dead are rising to eat the living. You need to make your way back home to your family outside the city, but the bridges and tunnels are clogged with traffic, mobile phones are inoperable, and mass transit is at a standstill. You are armed with a folding pocketknife.

What advantages do you have in this scenario?

_____

What are your disadvantages?

_____

How will you use your primary weapon?

_____

What is your tactical plan?

_____

ZOMBIE COMBAT TIP (MULTIPLE ATTACKERS): FIGHT OR FLIGHT

Facing a gang of flesh-eating ghouls can test even the most skilled combatants. Follow these tips to increase your odds of combat success:

1. Flee if you can; fight if you must.

2. Keep moving; do not stay stationary.

3. Do not allow yourself to be surrounded.

ZOMBIE COMBAT SCENARIO: THE OPEN ROAD

You and your team have been driven from your safe house by a mass of ghouls and are now on an open stretch of road. You hear moans of the undead in the near distance. According to your map, the nearest residence is ninety minutes away, and the sun sets in thirty minutes. In the haste of retreat, you failed to grab all your supplies, and you are without torches, candles, or firelighters. Your team is armed with a baseball bat, a fire axe, a crowbar, and a stiletto.

What advantages do you have in this scenario?

_____

What are your disadvantages?

_____

How will you use your primary weapons?

_____

What is your tactical plan?

_____

ZOMBIE COMBAT TIP (MULTIPLE ATTACKERS): CULLING THE HERD

When facing a group of ghouls, fight intelligently.

Outflank the group to avoid getting enveloped.

Pick off each attacker one at a time. Outflank again if necessary.

ZOMBIE COMBAT SCENARIO: THE AEROPLANE

Your city has been overrun by the undead. You are on a thirteen-hour direct flight to Tokyo's quarantined zone to meet up with your remaining family. In midflight, you are awakened by a noise up in the first-class cabin. It appears that several bitten passengers who made it past screening have turned and are now attacking the passengers. You are unarmed due to the security checks. There is a bar cart in the aisle.

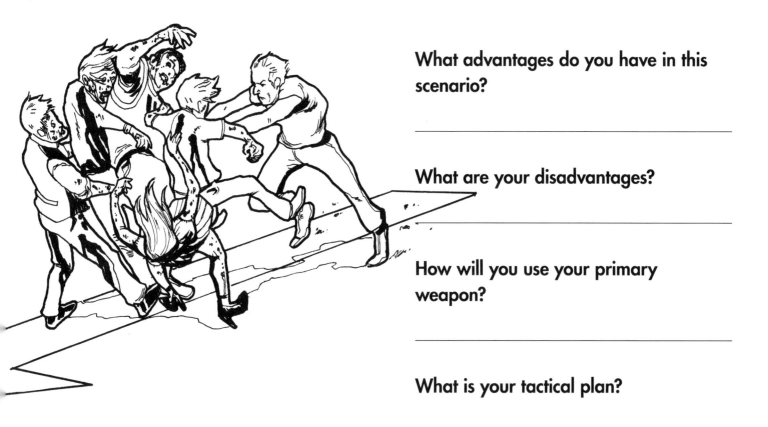

What advantages do you have in this scenario?

_____

What are your disadvantages?

_____

How will you use your primary weapon?

_____

What is your tactical plan?

_____

CLOSE-QUARTERS COMBAT TECHNIQUE: THE Q-TIP

TARGET AREA: Ear canal, brain

MOST EFFECTIVE WITH: Spiked weapons (ice picks, trench spikes, scratch awls)

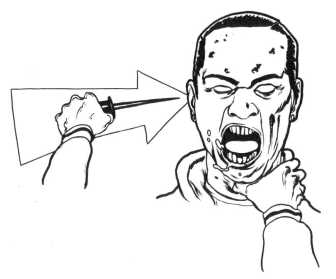

1. Draw your weapon and position it outside the ear cavity.

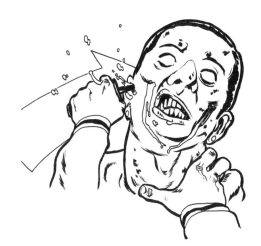

2. Forcefully thrust the weapon into the ear canal upwards towards the brain, driving the weapon to its hilt.

3. Twist the weapon, which aids in weapon extraction.

4. Extract the weapon vigorously and push the body away.

CLOSE-QUARTERS COMBAT TECHNIQUE: MIDDLE CRANIAL FOSSA (MCF) ATTACK

TARGET AREA: Underside of chin, soft palate, brain

MOST EFFECTIVE WITH: Edged weapons (combat knives, chef's knives, and screwdrivers)

1. Draw your weapon and position it so that the point rests directly under the ghoul's chin.

2. Drive the weapon straight up through the jaw into the brain. You will feel resistance once you puncture the soft and hard palates until you finally reach the brain. Keep driving the weapon upwards.

3. Forcefully retract your weapon to avoid catching it in the skull cavity.

4. Push the zombie away so its carcass does not fall on your body.

ZOMBIE COMBAT SCENARIO: THE KITCHEN

You find yourself in the kitchen of an abandoned home looking for supplies. The cutlery has been ransacked, but the cookware is untouched. Suddenly, five ghouls appear at the entrance to the room, blocking your only exit. A marble island separates you from the undead. You are unarmed.

What advantages do you have in this scenario?

_____

What are your disadvantages?

_____

How will you use your primary weapon?

_____

What is your tactical plan?

_____

UNARMED COMBAT TECHNIQUE: THE OUTSIDE SWEEP STOMP (OSS)

TARGET AREA: Outside thigh/calf region

TECHNIQUE: Unarmed technique designed to exploit your undead opponent's lack of balance

1. Mitigate the zombie's bite attack by securing its neck.

2. Hook one of your legs behind the ghoul's opposite leg. Remember that your throttling hand and hooking leg are on the same side (right hand throttle, right leg hook).

3. Aggressively smash your leg against the zombie's leg while simultaneously pushing against its neck, forcing the zombie's weight backwards. This should cause the ghoul to topple backwards to the ground.

4. Once the ghoul is on the ground, move towards its head and stomp on its skull with the heel of your shoe. It is recommended that you wear appropriate footwear in anticipation of this very purpose.

UNARMED COMBAT TECHNIQUE: THE INSIDE SWEEP STOMP (ISS)

TARGET AREA: Inside calf/ankle region

TECHNIQUE: Unarmed technique that works well if you notice the zombie standing with its legs far apart

1. Control the zombie's bite attack by securing its neck.

2. Place your foot between the ghoul's legs and hook your heel around its calf.

3. Sweep your leg back while pushing against its neck, forcing the zombie to the ground.

4. Quickly move towards the zombie's head and stomp on its skull with your heel.

MEDIUM-RANGE/MELEE COMBAT TECHNIQUE: STRACIRS TECHNIQUE

TARGET AREA: Temporal, nasal/orbital, or occipital regions

MOST EFFECTIVE WITH: Bludgeons (maces, hammers, clubs)

TECHNIQUE: Keeping clear of the zombie's primary threat zones (hands and mouth) while creating options for your own attack . . .

1. Strafe: Sidestep or "strafe" right or left out of the ghoul's fatal funnel.

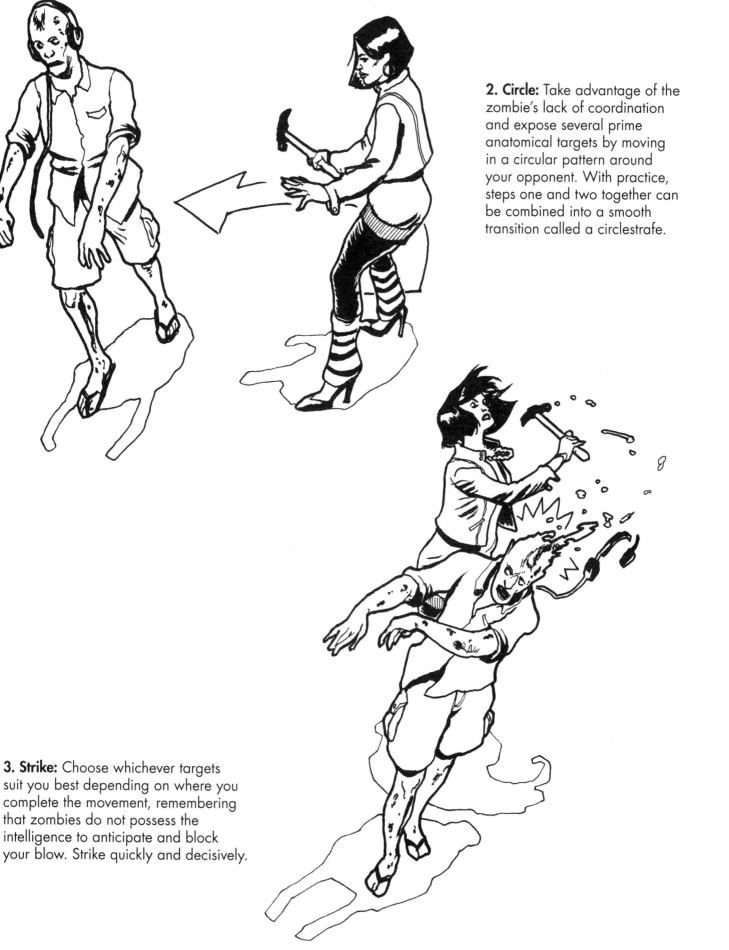

2. Circle: Take advantage of the zombie's lack of coordination and expose several prime anatomical targets by moving in a circular pattern around your opponent. With practice, steps one and two together can be combined into a smooth transition called a circlestrafe.

3. Strike: Choose whichever targets suit you best depending on where you complete the movement, remembering that zombies do not possess the intelligence to anticipate and block your blow. Strike quickly and decisively.

MEDIUM-RANGE/MELEE COMBAT TECHNIQUE: THE LUMBERJACK

TARGET AREA: Neck and throat region

MOST EFFECTIVE WITH: Bladed implements (swords, machetes, axes)

TECHNIQUE: "Notching" the neck to minimize the likelihood of losing the weapon . . .

1. Circlestrafe: Step out of the ghoul's fatal funnel.

2. Strike: Chop the neck with your blade, making sure you use an ample amount of force to inflict a deep, severe laceration.

3. Repeat: If your initial blow does not sever the head from its torso, do not panic. Circle approximately twenty-five degrees and strike your target a second time.

4. Finish: Repeat the preceding series of manoeuvres until your undead opponent's head is separated from its body. Remember, the severed head of a zombie requires a final terminating blow to the brain.

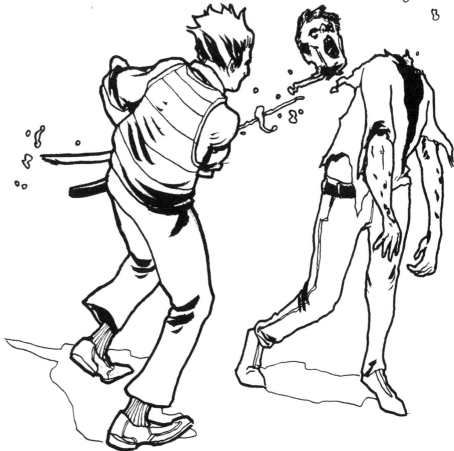

LONG-RANGE COMBAT TECHNIQUE: THE BLINDSIDE

TARGET AREA: Temporal region

MOST EFFECTIVE WITH: Heavy polearms and battle-axes

TECHNIQUE: While standing in front of your opponent:

1. Hold your weapon near the middle and end of the shaft with both hands.

2. Raise your weapon and pivot at the waist.

3. Strike the side of the skull in the region above the ear.

4. Follow through on your swing.

LONG-RANGE COMBAT TECHNIQUE: THE KEBAB

TARGET AREA: Middle cranial fossa (MCF)/underside of brain

MOST EFFECTIVE WITH: Stabbing/pointed polearms (spears, pikes, and lances)

TECHNIQUE: A difficult technique to execute, but perfectly suited to a long-range stabbing weapon

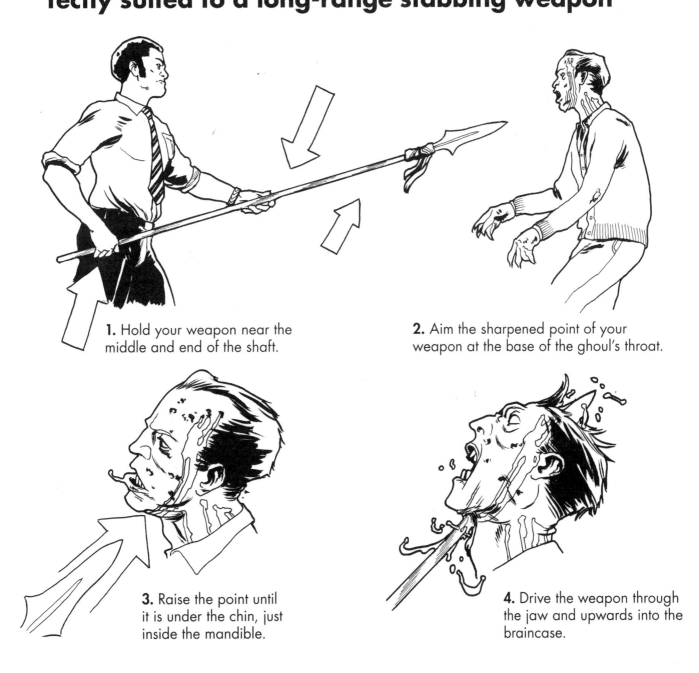

1. Hold your weapon near the middle and end of the shaft.

2. Aim the sharpened point of your weapon at the base of the ghoul's throat.

3. Raise the point until it is under the chin, just inside the mandible.

4. Drive the weapon through the jaw and upwards into the braincase.

LONG-RANGE COMBAT TECHNIQUE: THE MUSASHI

TARGET AREA: Neck/decapitation

MOST EFFECTIVE WITH: Bladed polearms, battle-axes, and great swords

TECHNIQUE: Similar to the blindside attack, with the exception of your final target

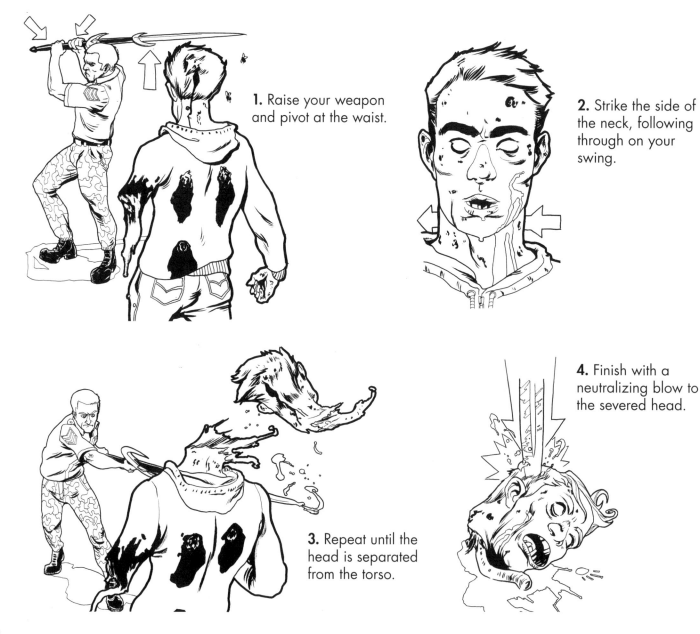

1. Raise your weapon and pivot at the waist.

2. Strike the side of the neck, following through on your swing.

3. Repeat until the head is separated from the torso.

4. Finish with a neutralizing blow to the severed head.

LONG-RANGE COMBAT TECHNIQUE: THE SKULLCAPPER

TARGET AREA: Nasal/orbital region

MOST EFFECTIVE WITH: Flat-bladed polearms (spades, shovels, and scrapers)

TECHNIQUE: While standing in front of your opponent:

1. Hold the weapon near the middle and end of the shaft.

2. Aim for the bridge of the nose.

3. Thrust forward aggressively, driving the blade through the skull.

4. Retract your weapon to ensure that it does not get stuck within the skull cavity. A powerful enough thrust can shear the top of a ghoul's head clean off.

ZOMBIE COMBAT SCENARIO: THE BARN

You and your partner wake in a bed of hay to the sound of the living dead pounding on the doors of the barn in which you took refuge during the night. Six ghouls push their way through the doors and begin to surround the two of you. Your only means of safety is the second-storey hayloft, but the ladder is on the other side of the barn. You are both armed with only combat knives, but a standard array of farm tools lies against the wall.

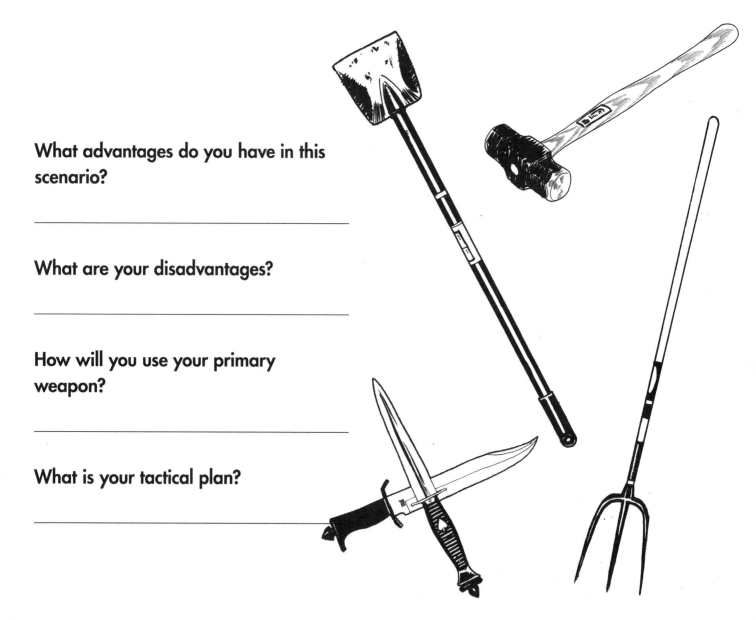

What advantages do you have in this scenario?

_____

What are your disadvantages?

_____

How will you use your primary weapon?

_____

What is your tactical plan?

_____

SOLUTIONS

PAGE 6—KNOW YOUR BLADES

Spear—Underside of chin

Zweihänder—Neck

Kukri—Neck and temple

Tomahawk—Temple

Folding Knife—Eyeball

Stiletto—Ear

SOLUTIONS FOR ZOMBIE COMBAT SCENARIOS:

You may be looking for solutions for the various scenarios presented throughout this field guide. You will not find any. The reason why is quite simple—there is no single "solution" for each of these scenarios. Every solution is dependent upon your individual strengths, weaknesses, and analyses of the situation. Compare your strategies with those of your friends, family, and teammates, and determine who made the most logical decision based on their specific assumptions and traits.